Holey, Wholly, Holy

A Lenten Journey of Refinement

Kris Camealy

Holey, Wholly, Holy
A Lenten Journey of Refinement

All scripture quotations, unless otherwise noted are taken from the Holy Bible, New International Version 1984®, NIV84® Copyright, 1984, by Zondervan Publishing House. Used by permission. All rights reserved.
Scripture quotations marked MSG are taken from The Message. Copyright © 1993, 1994, 1995, 1996, 2000, 2001, 2002. Used by permission of NavPress Publishing Group.
www.alwaysalleluia.com

Here is a trustworthy saying that deserves full acceptance: Christ Jesus came into the world to save sinners–of whom I am the worst. But for that very reason I was shown mercy so that in me, the worst of sinners, Christ Jesus might display his unlimited patience as an example for those who would believe on him and receive eternal life (1 Timothy 1:15-16).

For sinners like me—may we embrace the grace, that is ours in Christ.

Contents

Foreword
by Nikki Laven

Constant churning kept me up most nights. It was the nagging feeling I get when I have missed something important. Plus, I couldn't figure out why my mind was whirling with all things Lent related.

Growing up, the practice of Lent was not ingrained in me. Sure I knew enough to get by in casual conversation. I had given up things over the years and had often been creative in preparing my heart for the significance of Easter. Even now, as I sit and try, I can't think of an example worth sharing.

Maybe this year, God wanted me to forgo something substantial. More memorable. This I could do. I could bend lower and sacrifice more. Anything for guilt-free sleep. Only it never came.

Why did I have the impression my Savior wanted more from me? What was I missing and what was Lent all about, anyway?

My search engine led me on quite a maze. A road that led to confusion, more questions, and no answers whatsoever. Scary words like penance, repentance, self-denial, and fasting filled my screen. The further I dug, the more overwhelmed I became. This was not working for me.

I sat down at the dining room table instead, hoping to set my heart at ease. Armed with a notepad, pen, and Bible, I began to create my own map. With me at the starting point, the cross at the end, and Lent being the territory in-between. My goal was finding the best path for me. While reaching for my Bible, I recalled a verse I had read recently: "For Christ also suffered once for sins, the righteous for the unrighteous, to bring you to God. He was put to death in the body but made alive in the Spirit" (1 Peter 3:18 NIV).

It was the "Christ suffered...to bring you to God" part I couldn't get over. And I realized then and there I had always done it wrong.

Lent, for me, was always about what I would do for Christ. Me, sacrificing my way to the cross when really I should have focused on Him and how my Savior was going to bring me Home.

My path became clear. I disrobed my ideals, expectations, and all control in one prayer as I told Him I wanted to do whatever it took to become less so He could fill more of me. I was not prepared for what followed.

God held up a mirror, and I didn't even recognize myself. Seeing my raw, unedited heart brought shame to a whole new level. Amazing, the things I've held close for so long they appeared foreign when I was able to step back and truly see...me.

Then, I saw a reflection. A glimpse of what He sees in me and all we were working towards on this journey.

A part of me wants to spill my entire Lenten experience here. Share the ugly, the hard, and the glory found in-between. But this book is not for my story. And it's not about Kris's, either. This is about your season of refinement.

If you asked me to summarize my last Lenten experience, I would say that God stripped me down bare so He could clothe me in the way He'd always planned. And now, when I think of what Christ did for me on that cross, I take it personally. His love and grace came alive. Redemption turned intimate.

I'm actually looking forward to this Lenten season. Those words don't scare me anymore because I know now what awaits on the other side. And *Holey, Wholly, Holy* explains it brilliantly.

My mind keeps trying to imagine how my experience last year would have been different if I had been able to read this book before I began. It would have erased my confusion and aided in creating my map, that much is certain. I like to think it would have saved me some pain. I might have accepted grace sooner, and I am praying this holds true for you.

After reading, what surprised me most was how Kris knew my story so well. I had no idea what I was going through, but there is not one portion here He spared me from. I experienced each one. No shortcuts. Oh how I hope you will say the same.

Holey, Wholly, Holy is not a how-to book on doing Lent well. It's simply a companion's guide to help show you landmarks along the Lenten journey. With you at the starting point, armed with a mirror, and your redemptive self clad in righteousness at the end with a whole lot of you and Jesus in-between. Friend, let Christ bring you to God. This book will get you going in the right direction.

Some Notes Before We Begin

Holey, Wholly, Holy is intentionally not a 40 day devotional with scheduled readings for each day of Lent. Rather, it is my prayer that you will take your time reading through this book, searching the scriptures, and perhaps journaling your thoughts and insights along the way. My hope is that as you make your way through this season, you will ultimately find your place first, at the cross, and last, at the opening of the empty tomb, rejoicing in the resurrection.

My prayer for you, as we begin:
Father God, you are most perfect and Holy. We cannot fathom the depths of your love that sent your own Son through the horror and suffering of the crucifixion, in place of lowly sinners such as us. Lord as we search for our place alongside you this Lenten season, I ask that you would mercifully lead us into your will, that you would draw us ever closer to your heart, through your gentle humbling. Make us willing Father, help us to receive your grace. In Jesus' name I pray, Amen.

4

Why Lent?

Remember that "you are dust and to dust you shall return" (Genesis 3:19 NLT).

How many years have I walked that center aisle at the beginning of the Lenten season? How many times have I stood silent in line, waiting for the smudging of black ash across my forehead in the shape of a cross? Having grown up in the church, I figure I've made the journey at least 34 times. Even before I could walk, I likely experienced the marking while carried in my mother's arms.

Yet for all the times I've repeated the processional to the altar, the weight of the ashes never settled on me like it did last Lent—and I hadn't even attended the Ash Wednesday service. I found my face to the floor, the weight of the cross bearing down in a way I had never experienced. God stripped me down and, in doing so, brought me to the edge of myself.

This book is a result of that intense period of refinement.

A Brief History

The origin of Lent goes back to the time of the Apostles, and though the acceptable practices of the Lenten season have shifted over time, the idea behind the 40 days of Lent stands firm. Lent is traditionally observed for 40 days, from Ash Wednesday to Good Friday, excluding Sundays. The significance of the 40 days most commonly reminds us of the 40 days Jesus spent in the wilderness before the beginning of His short ministry on earth. As the church reflects on Jesus' 40 days in the wilderness, we are called to practice our faith in ways that stretch and bend us beyond what is comfortable. Generally during Lent, the Christian moves from a period of self-reflection, to confession, to repentance, and finally, to rejoicing in the grace of Christ's resurrection (Easter). In this book, I discuss these four subjects, beginning with self-reflection and culminating with the celebration of grace received through the risen Christ.

This is not meant to be a 40-day devotional, per se, but rather an aid in further reflection on the mystery and mercy of Jesus' death on the cross and His ultimate resurrection. My hope is that you find the readings encouraging and stirring as you draw closer to Christ during your own Lenten journey.

A Personal God

One of the most amazing things about God is how truly personal He is to each of us. Your Lenten journey will not look exactly like mine, and the struggles you face as you allow Him to refine you will be both unique to you as an individual and universal to all of us as members of the human race. It helps to remember that we face no temptation that Christ Himself has not faced:

> For we do not have a high priest who is unable to sympathize with our weaknesses, but we have one who has been tempted in every way, just as we are–yet was without sin. Let us then approach the throne of grace with confidence, so that we may receive mercy and find grace to help us in our time of need (Hebrews 4:15-16).

We should find it encouraging that not only does He know the weight of our struggles (and much more so) but He is also *with* us in the fires of refinement, just as He was with Shadrach, Meshach, and Abednego (Daniel 3:25). He walks with us in the flames and brings us through to the other side.

Come and Die

Traditionally, Lent involves a fast of some variety, with the object of the fast chosen by the practicing individual. Last year, I chose to fast from dessert. (I cringe just writing that.) As I look back at the work God did in my heart, I realize that often times we're only willing to give up the small things— soda, dessert, TV, alcohol, shopping and other completely unnecessary indulgences. The scripture that rung me out regarding what I'm willing to offer up was this one: "You do not delight in sacrifice, or I would bring it; you do not take pleasure in burnt offerings. The sacrifices of God are a broken spirit; a broken and contrite heart, O God, you will not despise" (Psalm 51:16-17).

It occurred to me that perhaps what God calls us to give up, really, is ourselves. The paltry offerings we prefer to give up, while they feel challenging, are perhaps less pleasing because we fail to give up the one thing that stands between us and Christ. Ourselves. Only when we have given up our own ambitions and desires, from that death to self, can we be used to produce much for His kingdom.

John 12:24 explains it this way: "I tell you the truth, unless a kernel of wheat falls to the ground and dies, it remains only a single seed. But if it dies, it produces many seeds."

Have you known the hard seasons of refining? If so, you likely recognize the burn of redemption as it begins to singe away the scales of the sinful life. We are called to live as Christ lived—willing to suffer as He suffered and to be stripped of the excesses and pride that prevent us from living a life that more fully glorifies Him. Dietrich Bonhoeffer said it this way, "When Christ calls a man, He bids him come and die"(Bonhoeffer 89).

As the church is traditionally stripped for the Lenten

season, so we, too, find ourselves naked before the Lord, shamed by our awareness of our weaknesses, constant stumbling, and self-righteousness. Jesus suffered all varieties of temptation in the wilderness, and as such, His faithfulness to the Father and His God-nature were put to test. Because He knew no sin (2 Corinthians 5:21), He endured a trial that we could never possibly endure apart from Him. On the cross He took on our shame, and His shame becomes our glory as we allow Him to clothe us in Himself.

In different ways, God tests our faithfulness. He refines us through trial and suffering so that when we emerge, we might better reflect His glory to the world. We live the Lenten season again and again throughout our lives, as God deals with our sins, and we confess and receive His forgiveness. Easter Sunday may occur once a calendar year, but it is experienced countless times in the Christian's life, as we repeatedly rejoice in the gift of our salvation through the death and resurrection of Jesus. By His good and generous mercy, we can endure hundreds of Lents in this life, as we remember these words found in Isaiah 48:10,11:

See I have refined you, though not as silver; I have tested you in the furnace of affliction. For my own sake, for my own sake I do this.....I will not yield my glory to another.

This is the hard refinement, the journey from holey (broken in sin) to wholly (surrendered) to *holy*.
The trials you endure, they are undeniably part of your story —but your life is not just about you—your life is about Christ in you—about the work He can do *through* you, when you yield to His will.

8

Introduction

Give up the struggle and the fight; relax in the omnipotence
of the Lord Jesus; look up into His lovely face and as you
behold Him, He will transform you into His likeness. You do
the beholding—He does the transforming. There is no shortcut to holiness. ~Alan Redpath

You Can't Hurry the Holy

Something about the incision site just didn't look right. Having been through two prior cesarean sections, I had a pretty good idea of what things ought to look like as they healed and this *definitely* wasn't right.

I knew a trip back to the doctor was in order. I also knew that I'd probably caused the problem by pushing myself too hard, too soon after surgery. I justified my increased activity levels because I had two other children who needed me, and well, I'm a mom—it's what I do.

Lying there, exposed on the exam table, I waited and wondered what the verdict would be. More stitches? Glue? Staples? What would it take to put me back together right?

The doctor gently poked a bit, eyed the incision site carefully, pulled a bottle of silver nitrate from the drawer and then looking up at me over the top of his glasses said, **"Take a deep breath and relax, this is gonna hurt."**

The Call

In Luke 4:23, Jesus calls himself "physician," and when we allow Him to, He heals us from the sin-sickness that separates us from Himself. This soul-healing, sanctification process requires endurance, patience, faith, and ultimate surrender to the cross of Christ. Christ calls us to meet Him in Gethsemane and pick up our own cross:

Whoever wants to be my disciple must deny themselves and take up their cross daily and follow me. For whoever wants to save their life will lose it, but whoever loses their life for me will save it. What good is it for someone to gain the whole world, and yet lose or forfeit their very self? (Luke 9:23-25).

Jesus calls us to holiness:

11

But just as he who called you is holy, so be holy in all you do; for it is written: "Be holy, because I am holy" (1 Peter 1:15-16).

Our life's purpose is to give God glory. We do that by reflecting His image to the world through our worship and our service to His kingdom. By His death He justified us, and through the refining fires He sanctifies us for the work of His purposes. But this refining is a process. You can't hurry the holy.

This book is a collection of short articles written along my own journey of refinement. Some of the writings have been adapted from my personal blog, AlwaysAlleluia.com, while others are entirely new. I pray you would be encouraged to continue through the fires of refinement and that the peace and joy of Christ would fully envelop you as you strive only to be closer to Him. You do not struggle in vain.

Friends, when life gets really difficult, don't jump to the conclusion that God isn't on the job. Instead, be glad that you are in the very thick of what Christ experienced. **This is a spiritual refining process, with glory just around the corner** (1 Peter 4:12-13, MSG, emphasis added).

Glory waits, just around the corner.

Self-Examination

(Holey)
I know, O Lord, that a man's life is not his own; it is not for a
man to direct his steps.
Jeremiah 10:23

It is this: that when we genuinely remember the death we
deserve to die, we will be moved to remember the death the
Lord in fact did die—because He took the place of ours.
Walter Wangerin, *Reliving The Passion*

There's No Shortcut to Holiness

In pursuit of Christ, we stumble into a scary town called *Redemption.* We all want to get there, but we prefer to come in the back alley rather than pass through the muddied streets under the glaring lights of self-reflection. The cross in the center of town calls our name, and some of us have scaled the edges of this place for years. We desperately want to get beyond it, but we're afraid—we know the path to redemption requires a trip through refinement.

Shame tells us to duck and cover. Sometimes, the ugly twins, *arrogance* and *pride,* hold us back. But the cross burns bright in the center of town; we find ourselves transfixed by the grace of it. Before we know it, we're taking one trembling step after another, hobbling nervously through the filthy streets of our darkest moments.

Shielding your eyes is useless. The only way to it is *through* it. On the road through Redemption we're forced to see the underbelly of our humanness, the struggle we pretend doesn't exist—the weaknesses we're afraid to show anyone. The blessing and challenge of the journey come through the revelations God gives us about ourselves—and our sins.

The road to Redemption is dangerous. All variety of pit-stops exist along the way, tempting us to linger where we shouldn't—depression, self-pity, unforgiveness, fear, anger, and a variety of other hollows beckon us off the main path.

We must remember, He walks *with* us—we don't pass through alone. Our silent companion holds our hand and leads us right up the middle of this place.

If you've skirted the edges of redemption and longed to get closer to Him, if you've hungered and thirsted for more of the Bread of Life, keep walking. Endure the pain of the refining process because when He has tested you, you will come forth as gold (Job 23:10, paraphrased). You are not

15

alone.

Choosing to Go

When we choose to go, to move closer to Jesus as we are called to do (1 Peter 2:21), we will eventually find ourselves stripped—naked before the Lord as we were intended to be. This process of moving closer, of growing in Christ, brings with it much pain. And while there's pain in the lessening of ourselves, the deeper blessings more than fill the holes we've spent years trying to cover over. God is big enough. His love is rich enough—but there is no shortcut. There is only the steady, trembling descent into the valley. The question He always asks is, will you go all the way with Him? Will you pursue holiness at the high cost of everything?

A.W. Tozer said, "Complacency is a deadly foe of all spiritual growth. Acute desire must be present or there will be no manifestation of Christ to His people. He waits to be wanted" (13).

Desiring God means we live an active faith, one that looks at a holey life and recognizes that grace can fill the holes. When we experience the fires that refine our faith, we can choose to go through them—to *grow* through them.

Coming Down

"We are brought down to the dust; our bodies cling to the ground. Rise up and help us; redeem us because of your unfailing love" (Psalm 44:25-26).

We begin collecting wounds and piling on scars from birth. Ejected from the safety of the womb, we immediately meet with a sinful world ripe with suffering. We grow and endure hardships of varying degrees from the mildly wounding to the most atrocious cruelty. We survive deep cuts and gashes and sometimes, if we can manage, we block the memories, and the pain dulls just enough.

But God has something better in mind. We can do more than simply limp along—His desire is for us to be complete. He longs to restore us, to strengthen us for the call He places on our lives.

In pursuit of life, of our own dreams, of our own magnificent imaginations, we have a knack for running right into the boiling furnace without even seeing it coming—"We sow on bright clear days the seed of our own destruction" (Capon 52).

God's desire for closer relationship with us requires us to be purified. Though He accepts us as we are, He has even better for us. He loves us too much to leave us in our mess. He collects our broken shards and creates beauty from mere fragments, but the process does not come without pain.

The truth of the Christian life is that we grow most in our faith through adversity. When our faces are pressed against the dirt, that's when our eyes are most open. The weight of the world presses us lower and it's there, in the spaces where we can scarcely breathe, that we find He is closest, holding our hands, lifting our spirits, filling up the holes in our cracked-up hearts.

17

Restoration is a process. It's not that He doesn't miraculously heal, certainly there's plenty of testimony to this kind of miraculous, instant healing. But for most of us, soul healing comes slowly—painfully.

You'll know it when He's calling you toward His refining fire. The smooth surface you've long stretched over, covering the cracks underneath, begins to ripple from the heat. Memories surface, old wounds begin to weep—the cracks widen and hurts spill.

This is not a time to turn and run, though that may be our instinct. This is the time to stand still, to listen to what He's whispering, and to allow Him to strip you of the covers you've been hiding under. Trust me when I say you've not got anything He hasn't seen before. Stand in this fire, let Him purify you—this is how He loves us. This is the process of sanctification.

Almost Forgotten

The memory surfaced out of nowhere. I'd read some other writer's words somewhere in the bowels of the Internet, and suddenly these old images began to fill my mind. It annoyed me, this unexpected intrusion of my past, and I fought hard to make the images stop—but they would not.

Without having to really even pray about it, I knew these memories resurfacing were from God. I can't really explain it, except that I knew it because the Holy Spirit whispered it somewhere in my hollowed-out-heart. I'd been seeking God harder these days, trying to uncover the reasons for some of my default behaviors. I'd been reluctant to ask Him because, honestly, self-examination is difficult at best and horrifyingly painful at worst. It had already been a bitter Lenten season for me and now, as the end was just a couple of weeks away, I just wanted rest.

God would give me rest, but on His terms and His timing. The memories hung around for days, no matter what efforts I made to block them out. All of my attempts to hide this from God only left me restless and on edge. I knew He was calling me to remember these difficult moments because there was something I needed to see that I hadn't seen at the time.

Finally after a few wrestling days, I relented. "What is it I need to see, Lord?" I demanded. The answer came immediately to mind. It suddenly made shocking sense.

Sometimes we are forced to remember our pasts in order to recover from the damage that has been done.

For years, I've struggled with feeling the need to perform to feel worthy. As I tried to lean into God during those long 40 days, something hung heavy on me, making it difficult to be near Him. I resisted my time with Him until His pull became too hard to ignore. Daily, I'd busy myself, trying

19

to dismiss the nagging feeling in my gut to go and sit with the Lord. My fear overcame me. What would He ask me to do? What if I didn't want to know? I have learned that once you acquire the truth, you are then responsible for action. I thought if I just stayed busy enough, God would go away and let me rest. What foolishness.

A Past Redeemed

He'd been pressing on me for weeks, and I recognized that the refining season wasn't through yet. As He called the images to my mind, I connected the dots. Each face I saw belonged to someone who had rejected me for my unwillingness to *perform* for them.

As a teenager, my budding faith and moral code prevented me from participating in activities which many of my peers chose to engage in. I suffered rejection multiple times as a result of my sensibilities. At the time, despite the pain of repeated rejection, I recovered quickly enough and moved on with my life. I didn't realize these experiences were changing the way I'd behave for years to come.

Yet God knew, and as I wrestled with feelings of failure as an adult, He set me free from the damage of the past. In His goodness, He filled the holes with His mercy and poured in truth to overtake the lies I'd grown to believe. This is the gift of surrender, this is newfound freedom in Christ—a past redeemed.

> Christ redeemed us from the curse of the law by becoming a curse for us, for it is written: "Cursed is everyone who is hung on a tree" (Galatians 3:13).

Ache

"But the way of Christ is cross bearing. Christ offers us resurrection power, and hence the hope of renewing rather than losing the old. But the renewal always involves crucifixion. Many of us are too comfortable to be willing." Vern Poythress

We fast from these little things, like dessert or caffeine, and we struggle and crave. Lent teaches us about sacrifice and we think it to be so hard, and while it is, because we are human and frail, our small giving-up is nothing compared to the ultimate sacrifice. Harder than the *fast,* is the turning of eyes inward, the sifting of filth that settles in the heart, *in my heart.*

When the shutters have been raised and the light pours in, the self-examination can feel a bit like medieval torture, a brutal pulling and stretching of a soul over the racks of truth. *Oh,* the brambles that have rooted there, and the indescribable ache in a spirit that has been wounded repeatedly by sins.

There's hollow space left behind when you give something up—a hole aching to be filled. Yet, here, in this painful, holey place—this is where the healing begins.

The renewal comes through the wringing out of the soul, through the pulling and dragging out of the ugly— through the sacrifice.

"… and by his wounds we are healed" (Isaiah 53:5).

Additional Scripture Reading

Joel 2:12-14
Mark 1:12-15
1 Corinthians 1:25-30
John 12:20-24

Confession

He who conceals his sins does not prosper, but whoever
confesses and renounces them finds mercy.
Proverbs 28:13

It is never fun to die. To rip through the dear and tender stuff
of which life is made can never be anything but deeply
painful. Yet that is what the cross did to Jesus, and it is what
the cross would do to every man to set him free.
A.W. Tozer

24

Get On Your Face

But he gives more grace. Therefore it says, "God opposes the proud, but gives grace to the humble" (James 4:6).

My baby girl says her evening prayers on her face and the first time she laid low to do it, I knew God was showing *me* something. Only days into it, Lent pushed me to the floor, the sheer weight of my struggle held me down for 40 days—a full immersion. A sputtering, choking confession, too long overdue. I'd prayed for resurrection but first there's the dying that *must* be endured.

God speaks, and I reluctantly heed. I live wracked with sin and a willful spirit that cracks back against the call to bend–to submit, *to surrender.*

Within the first week or two of the season, I'd consumed Brennan Manning's book, *All Is Grace.* His words tore me wide open and in the saline bath of confessional tears, I finally lived the baptismal immersion my soul had longed for and desperately needed.

God brought me right down, calling my face to the floor in a most uncomfortable position. These prideful knees resist bending. This Pharisee heart beats self-righteousness with each pulse, and I knew somewhere, *eventually*, the drop off would come.

Humility is a foreign land that speaks a language I haven't known. Love is humble and in living upright I question if I have ever really loved anything more than me. There are no bones about it, when I heard the firm whispers there in my closet, *indeed,* He told me to lay prostrate on the floor.

Here it is. The certain, *necessary* death, with my face pressed into carpet. I know I've lived a double life–one side of my mouth speaks about obedience while the other side

25

rallies for the independent spirit to "Go!" "Be!" "Do!" I didn't know Lent would kill me. *Thank God for the dying.* I find myself walking immersed, neck deep, continually splashing my face with the waters of this faith. Drinking it in, gulping it–gasping for it.

It's all grace and Manning said as much and lived the proof of it, a broken man living a cracked-up life, straddling the Truth and the *flesh.*

Dying to be remade requires confession. Confession of pride and failures dumped out into the light to be washed away into redemption's gutters, disappearing down drainpipes below. Beyond the confession, beyond the baptism and the receiving of forgiveness, awaits resurrection. This is the gift, the prize of the hard confessions.

I live, a new creation, fresh, wet–washed from the smears of a stiff-backed life.

Living full in Christ requires bent knees, bowed heads, humble hearts–*confession.* And in return He resurrects the dead, breathing new life where only a husk existed.

He is risen, and, in Him, we rise.

The God I have come to know loves me as much in a state of disgrace as He loves me in a state of grace, for His compassion is never, never, never based on our performance. It knows no shade of alteration or change. Jesus is the fulfillment of the Isaiah prophecy: the bruised reed of your life He will not crush, and the smoldering wick He will not quench, until He's led the truth of your life's story to victory. This night will you let Him come to you on His terms? Will you let Him love you as you are, and not as you should be? 'Cause nobody… is as they should be. (Brennan Manning, *All Is Grace)*

Let It Bleed

I'd prefer to be covered; I'm mostly comfortable with hiding. Most of us are.

But there comes a moment when the altar awaits, a beckoning to bare it all—to let the ugly spill out like the guts from a freshly slaughtered lamb.

We stand there, in the pool of it, with the freshness and warmth of the wound still dripping, still spilling–to let God into the mess. This is the hard confession.

We lay bare our hearts before the Lord, a cutting of sorts, allowing the poison to bleed out—healing will come.

For the wages of sin is death, and sin we have. We live as repeat offenders.

Christ crucified—the absolution for our sins. The sacrificial lamb, broken, poured out—chosen specifically for this purpose.

This is His gift. His sacrifice. We cannot fathom this love. This gift is undeserved, yet still, He's offered up, back broken open, skin raw and our sins bearing down, the weight of it all pressing, thorns piercing His head. He offers it even as we turn our backs and hide, as we disguise our weaknesses for the world—even as we pretend not to need this saving.

He bleeds, and we hide our faces. We are not worthy of this shedding. We don't want to know this, we don't want to see this–and yet we are called to die, to relinquish our very self. C.S. Lewis said of the crucifixion: "Christ died for men precisely because men are not worth dying for; to make them worth it."

We look for it now as we wander through the Lenten season–our sacrifice, our learning to die to sin to live with him. We spill the ugly to allow Him to heal the wounds— replacing bits of us with pieces of Himself.

We lift hands and praise Him, as what was once hidden

is now revealed.

We learn to walk truthfully, no longer damming up the floodgates. We rip the cord and hold on as our true identity gushes out of us—our weaknesses, our failings, our stumbles and our wanderings. All of this, that we might learn to live authentically, honestly before Him, before *each other.*

There is no shame in brokenness. We are all shattered pieces of the body, just trying to heal up and close the holes that sin leaves behind. Replacing the darkness with light. Hope lives. Resurrection awaits.

Brave

I thought that brave meant never giving up. Brave, to me, meant fighting to the death. In a moment of divine intervention I got this message from my friend, she said one word: surrender.

She didn't know how I needed that word. She didn't know the wrestling I'd been doing with God, or how, as her message lit up the screen in my hand, my heart and soul ached with the weight of original sin. Her word pierced straight through and my shoulders sagged as the word burrowed deep. *Surrender.*

I had fought hard that week. Fought both God and the enemy, a tug-of-war match for the books. I limped into the weekend.

Sometimes bravery looks more like surrender. How on earth this can be I don't fully know, but like everything else in God's economy that runs backwards and inside out to the way *I* think it should, this somehow makes sense.

I'd grit my teeth and dug in my heels and flat out refused and that one word cracked me wide open at five-thirty on a Thursday afternoon. When it comes to walking closer with Christ, my charging ahead, insisting on braving the way on my own terms isn't bravery, it's foolishness. It's willful disobedience.

To walk closer with Christ, we must bravely surrender to His will, to His discipline, to our independent selves who insist that we can handle life on our own, *thankyouverymuch.* Turns out, surrendering is harder than bravely pushing ahead.

Your attitude should be the same as that of Christ Jesus:Who, being in very nature God, did not consider equality with God something to be grasped, but made himself nothing, taking the very nature of a servant,

29

being made in human likeness. And being found in appearance as a man, he humbled himself and became obedient to death–even death on a cross! (Philippians 2:5-8)

Coming Clean

The upheaval of a comfortable life slips in sometimes without notice at first. An unexplained attitude of irritation and tightness of lips, of fists. The Holy Spirit begins to whisper and, like children, we stick our fingers in our ears and flap our tongues in an effort to block it out. *We know what's coming.*

The slow burn of sanctification melts away the edges, and as the fire slips in, we begin to crack. A confession swells and resisting will only lead to more pain. *We must bend.*

His Word tell us this process is how He *really* loves us. By loving the filth right out of our hearts, He draws us ever closer and when we release, when we lay low, we can finally hear His heartbeat. Because, when we are lying down in the pit, it's His face we see pressed into the dirt beside us.

Lent sometimes comes wrapped in filthy paper with tattered ribbons, sin bound so tight—barbed-wire piercing holes into a heart in need of a good bleed. We must wrestle out the ugly that has for years made a home in the dark festering places.

Reading the words over the Seder meal, *"yeast leavens or puffs up, as pride and sin inflates our hearts..."* Pride prevents the confession. Pride pushes back grace from whitewashing the muddied up walls we crudely erect within our hearts. I read Luke 14:11, and I wail: *"For everyone who exalts himself will be humbled, and he who humbles himself will be exalted."*

It doesn't matter that Lent lasts just 40 days. The refining process runs life-long. God knows no timetable except that which He sets by His own hand. He will press us until we come clean. He woos us through flame, with passion and persistence.

31

The grace of it is that, through the scalding, we become renewed. The Father grafts new skin to cover old wounds, and in time we gain wisdom and strength. We become healthier, holier, a little bit more like Christ, and less like us. That is our highest calling. I'll live in the fires of refinement, if that's what it takes.

The Crushing Place

The first time I remember confessing anything, I sat across the desk from an old Catholic priest who has neither a face nor a name in my memory. As my "First Communion" drew closer, this apparently was part of the preparation—a face-to-face confession of my sins. I can't recall what I confessed, if anything. I don't remember much besides that.

This memory exists for me in the form of yellow-edged snap-shots from the early 1980s. The memories are mostly still, paused moments of a season when I'm certain life for my parents with three young children was anything but still. But I do recall the awkwardness of this forced confession. I remember the way I shifted uneasily in a giant chair that further dwarfed my seven-year-old self, my toes in black patent leather dangling, swaying nervously above the floor. I remember the shame I felt.

It's been years since that day, and I've racked up thousands of sins since that Sunday. I've deliberately turned my back on God in willful seasons of civil disobedience to His word, to His calling. I've pressed my palms hard flat against my ears and stood with my nose to the wind in blind oblivion to the whirl of the *Spirit* whipping through my life. I'm good at tightening my lips and clenching my jaw locked-tight.

Confession smelts and causes us to change. True confession comes without coercion. Honest confession before God comes only when the scales have slipped from our hearts and we know, we really *see* the dark places where we've gone awry. Like our cheap fasts, I'm certain God's not all that interested in our compelled confessions when we are not truly moved in our hearts to lay low before Him. After all, the Lord does not look at the things man looks at. "Man looks at the outward appearance, but the Lord looks at the heart" (1

33

Samuel 16:7).

Christ had no confession of sins to make. He knew no shame except ours because He bled innocent blood in place of the likes of me. But confession isn't purely for the remission of sins. Confession, as Christ demonstrated in the garden, was a time of emptying before the Lord all that terrifies and troubles us. Confession is a conversation where we remember that He is over all, and our place is under Him.

Before His crucifixion, Jesus spent a night slumped over in desperate prayer, in a garden where this whole story began. Except this garden isn't a paradise on earth. Rather, this garden is named for the pressure of production. This garden is named for the place where fruit dies to become something else. *Gethsemane.*

I read in *Strong's* that the word Gethsemane means "the crushing place" or "place where oil is pressed," and the irony (or appropriateness) of such a place setting the scene for Jesus' last night on earth is not lost on me. It's there in this crushing place where Christ shed crimson tears not of water, but of holy blood. His anguish, so intense that as a man He questions the necessity of His impending death, and yet, as the Christ, He simultaneously accepts it out of His perfect obedience to the Father.

As we wander through this Lenten season, we may (and hopefully will) find ourselves at the crushing place. This is a place not for fear, but for freedom. Confession of our doubts and struggles loosens the chains of sin and sends us further into the fires of refinement and deeper on our journey of sanctification. Here in this place, we weep with the anguish of a soul that has seen the depths of our own depravity. We weep with Christ, with honest sorrow and ridiculous joy so that, as we let it all out, we will walk out of the garden freer than when we stumbled in. He takes our filth and nails it to a tree, and the gift is ours when we confess—humbly confess.

"Forgive us our sins, for we also forgive everyone who sins against us. And lead us not into temptation" (Luke 11:4).

Additional Scripture Reading

Luke 11:1-9
Mark 14:32-51
Hebrews 12:6-8
1 John 1:9
Proverbs 28:13
Psalm 51:1-5

Repentance

This is what the Sovereign Lord, the Holy One of Israel, says:
"In repentance and rest is your salvation, in quietness and
trust is your strength, but you would have none of it."
Isaiah 30:15 NIV

But the man who is not afraid to admit everything that he sees
to be wrong with himself, and yet recognizes that he may be
the object of God's love precisely because of his
shortcomings, can begin to be sincere. His sincerity is based
on confidence, not in his own illusions about himself, but in
the endless, unfailing mercy of God.
Thomas Merton, *No Man Is An Island*

All or Nothing

"And anyone who does not take his cross and follow me is not worthy of me. Whoever finds his life will lose it, and whoever loses his life for my sake will find it" (Matthew 10:38-39).

"When Christ calls a man, He bids him come and die. It may be a death like that of the first disciples who had to leave home and work to follow Him, or it may be a death like Luther's, who had to leave the monastery and go out into the world. But it is the same death every time—death in Jesus Christ, the death of the old man at his call" (Bonhoeffer 44).

When God kindly asks us to set down our bundle of *wants*, it's not likely that we refuse Him outright. Rather, we're often very good at pretending to submit while grabbing for the goods when we think He's not looking. With fingers crossed behind our back, we live as if we can operate outside the scope of His vision. The truth is, He doesn't just want our bag of dreams and longings. His desire is for us to be wholly His, that He might make us holy for Him.

With God it's all or nothing. Loving God halfway is the same as not loving Him at all. Loving Him out of mere obligation is equally useless. In Matthew 12:30, Jesus says it this way, "He who is not with me is against me, and he who does not gather with me scatters." This is hard for us because we tend to ride the fence. We want the blessings without the work. We want the good life without the commitment to maintaining it. We want to win the lottery rather than earn our living.

It's much the same with our faith—with our desire for redemption. We want the gold without the fire—the resurrection without the horror of the cross. But His words are clear. "For [His] sake, we face death all day long" (Psalm

44:22). The only way to get closer to Him is to lie down and die with Him. Daily. When we're stagnant in our faith that usually means it's time to die. Don't worry, resurrection is coming.

> In all this you greatly rejoice, though now for a little while you may have had to suffer grief in all kinds of trials. These have come so that the proven genuineness of your faith—of greater worth than gold, which perishes even though refined by fire—may result in praise, glory and honor when Jesus Christ is revealed. Though you have not seen him, you love him; and even though you do not see him now, you believe in him and are filled with an inexpressible and glorious joy, for you are receiving the end result of your faith, the salvation of your souls (1 Peter 6-9).

Feasting and Fasting

I've heard many people say they have trouble fasting because of their "issues with food." And I understand this. *I do*. Food in our culture is far more than sustenance that keeps us upright and moving. Food is entertainment, it's medicine, it's a lover and a friend in the dark of our days when we find ourselves desperately scratching for things to fill the holes. Yes, I'd say we have issues with food.

I find it interesting Satan used food to tempt Eve— food as the mystical elixir that would crown us in glory and knowledge. Poisonous, forbidden food, and yet she ate– sharing her sin with her husband and the rest of us.

Fasting is a practice not to be taken lightly. It is a spiritual discipline that requires sacrifice, and for some the sacrifice weighs harder than for others. But fasting isn't about food. Fasting is about faith. It is about consciously choosing Christ when we want nothing more than to stuff ourselves with that which is temporary.

Jesus *knew* temptation. He knew how delicious food looked from His rock in the wilderness, Him with His stomach 40 days empty, rumbling, mouth salivating for something He could sink His teeth into. He knew it and yet He resisted. "After fasting 40 days and 40 nights, he was hungry. The tempter came to him and said, 'If you are the Son of God, tell these stones to become bread.' Jesus answered, 'It is written: 'Man shall not live on bread alone, but on every word that comes from the mouth of God.' " (Matthew 4:2-4).

The Bread of Life

We find fasting difficult because we have grown unaccustomed to the hollow feeling in our bellies. We fill our empty with various *things*, food or otherwise—*anything* to mute the pangs that rise up and remind us of our unworthiness, our incompleteness apart from the Father. We gasp, parched and weary and in our soul-starved state, we willingly consume whatever looks good—whatever the tempter dangles in front of our eyes. Still, despite the filling, we live starving.

Apart from Christ, we will make this mistake again and again. On our own we *cannot* resist. We all stumble and fall short, yet Jesus set the example for us by repeatedly denying the temptations to be more, have more, consume more. We cannot live by bread alone. We need more and this is the very lie we tell ourselves when we say that we cannot *fast*. But Christ says He is the bread of Life. We say, *He's not enough.*

We turn and resist the very spiritual practice that will nourish us in a way we cannot fully understand. We deny the words of Philippians 4:13: I can do everything through Him who gives me strength.

God sets the spiritual table and invites the malnourished:

"Come, all you who are thirsty, come to the waters; and you who have no money, come, buy and eat! Come, buy wine and milk without money and without cost" (Isaiah 55:1).

He rings His celestial dinner bell and calls us to Himself. He asks nothing, other than that we come- *without money, without cost*, He implores:

"Listen, listen to me, and eat what is good, and you will delight in the richest of fare" (Isaiah 55:2).

He calls us to come to Him and to eat what is good, what is rich and *satisfying*. Why not come to Him? Allow yourself to come empty, refraining from that which only gives temporary satisfaction, and let Him fill you.

"For he satisfies the thirsty and fills the hungry with good things" (Psalm 107:9).

While fasting is a spiritual discipline with much biblical support, some struggle with health concerns that make fasting from food dangerous or perhaps even impossible. Fasts need not be limited to food. Consider your situation, and perhaps consult your physician and determine what you can safely fast from. While we may think of a fast as torturous, the intent is not to cause suffering or illness, but rather that in the absence of the object of our fast, we would draw closer to Christ as we lean into Him for strength. Remember, your heart behind the fast is what matters, not the fasting itself.

For further readings on fasting, see Psalm 69:10, Ezra 8:21-23 Daniel 10:3, Jonah 3:5-10, Isaiah 58:1-14, and Matthew 6:16-18.

Turn

If we claim to be without sin, we deceive ourselves and the truth is not in us. If we confess our sins, he is faithful and just and will forgive us our sins and purify us from all unrighteousness. If we claim we have not sinned, we make him out to be a liar and his word has no place in our lives (1 John 1:8-10).

My sense of direction is horrible at best. Add my independent spirit to the mix, and it's no mystery as to how I easily lose my way in certain seasons. At some point, I lost my way. I turned left instead of right, and I stood up too tall when I should have been bent low. I probably made a hundred tiny, seemingly insignificant decisions that nudged me further from the throne. Isn't that how it goes? We live overcome with decisions to make, laziness grabs the wheel, fear slams foot to the floor, and without full awareness we're quickly lost.

Rather than quietly seeking refuge, I stood arrogant and prideful against the Refiner's fires. Even in writing it, my foolishness insults my own knowledge of what is best. I'm not proud of it, but it's the truth.

While I've hungered for transformation, still I sometimes stand with my heels dug in against the sand, willfully disobedient against getting up, picking up my mat– taking the leap.

How is it possible to forget the character of God? Sin. Deceit. Sour life experiences. These bitter roots cloud the clearest vision when allowed to root and grow in the dark cracks. Despite trying to live life worshiping, the very face of the One I worshiped faded, and slowly my own baggage nearly eclipsed it completely.

Lift up your voice with a shout, lift it up, do not be

afraid; say to the towns of Judah,"Here is your
God!" (Isaiah 40:9)

Chasing dreams, following the rules, doing the work—
this distracted me from pursuing Him, and then I flat forgot
exactly who He is. I've read Isaiah 40 every day this week.
Every time I read it, I wept–

"He tends his flock like a shepherd: He gathers the
lambs in his arms and carries them close to his heart;
he gently leads those that have young" (Isaiah 40:11).

The poetry and power used to describe God in this
chapter is nothing short of awe-inspiring and deeply
humbling.The humbling is what I've needed, the awe is what
I'd lost.

"Who has measured the waters in the hollow of his
hand, or with the breadth of his hand marked off the
heavens?" (Isaiah 40:12)

One day last summer, my littles and I picked a handful
of caterpillars off of our broccoli. The kids begged to keep
them, so we did. They sat in a jar for a couple of days, and
then we watched as their movement slowed and their shape
transformed. Three days after collecting them they all slept
soundly in their cocoons, transformation in the works.

"He sits enthroned above the circle of the earth, and its
people are like grasshoppers. He stretches out the
heavens like a canopy, and spreads them out like a tent
to live in" (Isaiah 40:22).

Once the caterpillars had no where to go, it seemed

there was nothing left to do but let the process begin. At some point, we have to yield to the Father and let Him work in us. We must turn to Him.

"Do you not know? Have you not heard?
The Lord is the everlasting God, the Creator of the ends of the earth. He will not grow tired or weary, and his understanding no one can fathom" (Isaiah 40:28).

Two weeks later, we set 10 butterflies free. I watched hopeful as they lifted off to places they'd never have seen from the ground. Fighting against Him prevents us from experiencing all that He has for us. There's a season for both scrimping along on your belly and fluttering your wings to go higher.

Metanoeó

"But unless you repent, you too will all perish" (Luke 13:3).

I've wondered sometimes what true repentance looks like. Repentance often follows the confession—at least it must if the confession is to have been worthwhile. The Greek word Jesus used for repent is *metanoeó*, which literally means, "think differently after."

The fruit of a heart that seeks unity with Christ is a change of perspective. As we wander through the Lenten season, our contemplation of the cross should transform our hearts. The hope is that we would come to think differently than before. The truth is, coming face to face with the reality of a crucified Christ *does* change our minds. We can no longer look on the cross as a mere symbol of a mythological tale of supposed salvation.

When we imagine our Jesus hanging on that tree, nails split right through His hands and the crown pressed deep into His scalp, bleeding and oozing, when we look on His body there lashed within a fraction of life, skin barely clinging to the bones, muscles exposed and torn from the strain and stretching—we cannot help ourselves but to think differently. Gazing upon the cross we find our own place in this story. We realize that our view is that of the thief hoisted up there next to Him. We find our identity in the soldiers who mocked Him and in the crowd who demanded His blood and rallied hard for His death. We see that we are not mere spectators in His suffering and death, but in fact are the cause of it.

Walter Wangerin reminds us: "When we genuinely remember the death we deserve to die, we will be moved to remember the death the Lord in fact did die—because His took the place of ours" (Wangerin 22).

We come away from this scene with a hunger to live as

47

He lived. Paul writes in Ephesians 5:1-2: "Be imitators of God, therefore, as dearly loved children and live a life of love, just as Christ loved us and gave himself up for us as a fragrant offering and sacrifice to God."

This living as Christ exemplifies our repentance and reveals a mind and heart transformed—that we would no longer live as those hiding from the fires of refinement, but would instead fling ourselves willingly into His furnace. We can trust Him to bring us forth sanctified, redeemed for His purposes.

There is no greater glory than a life lived to honor the Lord. Tozer said, "The man who has God for His treasure has all things in one" (Tozer 14).

May we never strive for anything other than a life marked by repentance, may we go forward from this Lenten season thinking differently than before.
Metanoeó.

Additional Scripture Readings

Ezekiel 33:11
Luke 24:47
2 Peter 3:9
Matthew 3:1-8

Atonement

(Holy)

His divine power has given us everything we need for life and godliness through our knowledge of him who called us by his own glory and goodness. Through these he has given us his very great and precious promises, so that through them you may participate in the divine nature and escape the corruption in the world caused by evil desires. 2 Peter 1:4

God the Holy One is the source of life; sinfulness separates us from the holiness and so separates us from life. Holiness is a return to Eden's ideal and a taste of paradise. The holy life is a foretaste of heaven on earth. It is not God's burden for us but God's best for us. Simon Ponsonby

Anything

The hard refining had begun to ease, the heat grew less intense and as I thumbed through an old journal, I saw the words I'd scrawled out, "Lord remove my pride." I'd forgotten that prayer. I mean, I've muttered and wept and sighed a great many prayers in my life, I can't possibly recount them all, and yet, God never forgets a one of them.

All this time with my face in the carpet I didn't know He was answering a prayer. He's dependable. In His omnipotence He chooses when and how to fulfill the cries of a heart that longs for Him.

I'd prayed the "anything prayer," the one that says "have your way with me Lord, do anything that would bring you glory." Had I not believed He would? Or maybe I believed but imagined the process would be cleaner, less painful, less heartbreaking. His ways are not our ways, and when our life is so rapt with our selfish ambitions, we don't always let go neatly.

What we can't always see in the heat of change in progress is the glory that awaits. I wasn't actively seeking refinement. God chose the time and process according to His purposes and not my own. A great many times in our Christian life we will endure hard times. Those times are always a preparation for the next thing. The unseen.

We are no good to God when we're playing God ourselves. How can we serve and love and reflect Christ when we begin and end with ourselves? The refinement is not to be feared or resisted. We can walk willingly into the fires because He's already been there, He goes there still. What we find in the lower places of repentance is a God who knows us with all of our ugly on the inside and yet He cups our faces in the filth and lifts us. He lifts us up as we set the weight of the baggage we carry down.

The journey through Lent is a journey that doesn't end at the cross. *No!* This journey ends at the empty tomb when we realize that He's beaten back death. This journey ends in the victory of grace for sinners and redemption for those who believe. We find Jesus walking on the road and comforting those who mourn. We find Him with pierced hands outstretched encouraging us to poke our own fingers into His holy spaces and see that He is real—that He lives and because He lives, *we live.*

In resisting the cross, in running from time in the tomb, we risk missing the greatest glory that ever existed—resurrection. There's no greater hope than knowing that in time, we will be raised with Him—on earth, as it is in heaven. He picks us up from the ashes, as one journey ends a new one begins. Your hard refinement is not the end, but rather a new beginning. He's calling you out for more than this. He's preparing you for glory, friends, for *His* glory.

Wear the Robe

I delight greatly in the Lord; my soul rejoices in my God. For he has clothed me with garments of salvation and arrayed me in a robe of righteousness, as a bridegroom adorns his head like a priest, and as a bride adorns herself with her jewels (Isaiah 6:10).

Wearing holy righteousness feels sometimes like a robe that doesn't fit. Knowing the depths of my depravity, I recognize my inferiority. But that's precisely the point. As the sun rises on the empty tomb, we discover a Christ who overcomes the hindrance of death to proclaim everlasting life.

We find through Him this same offer extended to us, and in fact it's more glorious because while He took on death which He never deserved, we deserve eternal punishment and can escape it. In His generous mercy, He offers to cover our sins with His holy robe.

Grace overtakes a sin-wrecked life and makes us holy. I wrestled this grace to the ground and I'm thankful to say that because I lost, I won. After a hard season of refining, where God repeatedly revealed my broken places, I couldn't bear the weight of this undeserved covering. My shame was too great, as was my pride.

In humility, we must allow Him to drape it over us. No, we don't deserve it. We can't afford it, for the cost is innocent blood shed for its purchase—and yet it's ours for the taking. What glory! What grace!

We can endure the process of sanctification because we are called to *live*. God is the source of all life and thus He calls us to Himself. We could not bridge the gap if not for the crucified Christ.

Alleluia! He lives, and in Him we live!

The God who made the world and everything in it is the Lord of heaven and earth and does not live in temples built by hands. And he is not served by human hands, as if he needed anything, because he himself gives all men life and breath and everything else. From one man he made every nation of men, that they should inhabit the whole earth; and he determined the times set for them and the exact places where they should live. God did this so that men would seek him and perhaps reach out for him and find him, though he is not far from each one of us. 'For in him we live and move and have our being.' As some of your own poets have said, 'We are his offspring' (Acts 17:24-28).

By His Strength, For His Glory

Some time ago, I started signing things with this little phrase, "by His strength, for His glory." In my desperate prayers to be more like Him, less like me, I realized (or rather perhaps God revealed to me) that the only way to redemption is by His strength, and it's always for His glory. Not only is this the only path to redemption, but it's also the only way worthy of living the Christian life.

As we grow through our refining, we realize that we live and breathe because of His grace, not our goodness or ability. Our life exists because he breathed it into purpose by His own strength, and for His ultimate glory. As "little Christs," we're called to live as examples of God's love on earth—a light for the world, the salt of the earth.

Living redeemed is impossible without the strength of Christ in us. It's not for our own glory we serve, but rather for His glory, that all might see Him in us and praise Him, rather than us. We're to be a mirror reflecting the true source. 1Peter talks about this in reference to how we ought to use our gifts to serve:

Each one should use whatever gift he has received to serve others, faithfully administering God's grace in its various forms. If anyone speaks, he should do it as one speaking the very words of God. If anyone serves, he should do it with the strength God provides, so that in all things God may be praised through Jesus Christ. To him be the glory and the power for ever and ever. Amen. (1 Peter 4:10-11)

He refines us that we might shine brighter for *Him.*

And it's by His strength, for His glory—because ultimately it isn't about us. We endure the hard refining for the Father's glory, as it says here in John:

"He cuts off every branch in me that bears no fruit, while every branch that does bear fruit, he prunes so that it will be even more fruitful. This is to my Father's glory that you bear much fruit showing yourselves to be my disciples." (15:2,8)

I've wrestled continually with this prickly temptation to turn everything around to be about me. This is the reason I blame others for my struggles and shirk difficult responsibilities—this is the reason I battle selfishness and pride. Even when the refining process first noticeably began last year, I tried again and again to make it about me. But it isn't. God doesn't just purify us so we'll be a better wife, or friend, or mother. Those are more side-effects than purpose. He prunes us so we will bear fruit. For Him. For His kingdom, not ours. Our faith is purified so that God will be glorified.

Praise be to the God and Father of our Lord Jesus Christ! In his great mercy he has given us new birth into a living hope through the resurrection of Jesus Christ from the dead, and into an inheritance that can never perish, spoil or fade—kept in heaven for you, who through faith are shielded by God's power until the coming of the salvation that is ready to be revealed in the last time. In this you greatly rejoice, though now for a little while you may have had to suffer grief in all kinds of trials. These have come so that your faith—of greater worth than gold, which perishes even though refined by fire—may be proved

genuine and may result in praise, glory and
honor when Jesus Christ is revealed (1 Peter 1:3-7).

Obviously God wants us to be the best people we can
be. He wants us to love our families and neighbors as He
loves them. But even that isn't about us. Loving like Christ
means loving selflessly, even unto death. The only way to get
it right is to give the glory to Him. The call to refinement for
the Christian is not about making us look better, it's about us
reflecting Christ better.

Redemption's a dirty town. The filth of our lives piles
up in the gutters and some days, we sell little bits of our soul
to avoid walking through it. But there's only one way to the
other side, and every alley ends up the same place. For most
of us, Redemption's a ghost town, a desert that ought to be
crossed in a few days, but some of us will take years to get
through. It's not a race. There's no rushing the process along.
Obedience is critical, humility necessary, and prayer and
communion are the sustenance for the journey.

If you're walking this road and need some company,
I'd love to hear from you. Email me at
kris@alwaysalleluia.com or find me on Twitter
(twitter.com/kriscamealy) and Facebook
(facebook.com/krisecamealy)

I know how hard this path can be, but I've also seen
glimpses of glory and there's joy and hope along the way—
keep your eyes on Him.

"Dear friends, do not be surprised at the painful trials
you are suffering as though something strange were
happening to you, but rejoice that you participate in
the sufferings of Christ, so that you may be overjoyed
when his glory is revealed" (1 Peter 4:12).

Acknowledgements

Thank you always feels too small a phrase for the amount of support and encouragement I receive from those in my inner circle. So for lack of a better expression of gratitude, and too small of a budget to throw each of these dear people their own individual party, I offer up my deepest thanks to...

My husband, Kurt, and my children. You always support me in everything I set out to do. Your quiet strength and encouragement have been the very things that have held me up on some of my most difficult days, Thank you for loving me like Jesus loves me—in spite of all my faults. My children, you are so little right now, but you have played such pivotal roles in my spiritual journey thus far. My prayer is that you will always find your place at Jesus' feet, and that you will never be afraid to walk through the fires with Him. I can't wait to see what God teaches us next.

My parents, for loving me with freedom and not stifling my middle-child ways, for encouraging me to write from when I was young, and for taking me to church and introducing me first to God and Lent and eventually to this Jesus who turns our world upside down again and again. You two have played an instrumental role in helping me to become the person I am today, working tirelessly to instill in me the values I hold dear, and always encouraging me to just keep going. I love you and am truly grateful I was born unto you, for such a time as this.

My dear siblings, James and Seana, for never making me feel foolish for chasing my dreams. We've always been a team, even as children, even when we didn't understand each other as adolescents, you've always been on my side, and for that I am eternally grateful.

Michelle P., Carrie B., Jana D., and Christine H., you

are my inner circle—the ones who both have held me accountable and prayed faithfully for me in all my various endeavors. I am certain I wouldn't have written a word of this, if not for your prayers and friendship. You are the most beautiful representation of Christ to me.

Christine Heister, thank you so much for the beautiful soul-art you created for this book. You masterfully translated the heart of my words into images, and I am so grateful for the way you *see* Jesus.

Thank you, to my HelloMornings accountability friends: Aurie, Larri, Julie, Lauren, Lisa, and Rebecca. I am certain this book would not have come together if not for your constant prayers and encouragement. You helped me start my day at Jesus' feet and so many times your prayers carried me through. I am deeply grateful and forever blessed by what you have helped me accomplish.

Evelyn, Thank you for your faithful coaching and support. You were there when this started and you have seen me through to this point. Your support and spiritual counsel have been gifts I never imagined. Thank you for taking the time each week to speak with me. I treasure our talks.

Nikki, my friend. Thank you for walking the hard path to redemption with me. Thank you for holding my hands and listening to my heart, for letting me bleed the ugly right out, without fear of judgment or shame. I am so grateful for the wild ways God has woven you into my life. Your willingness to bare your own heart a bit in the foreword of this book is a testament of how gracious and generous you are.

Sarah, thank you for taking the time to edit this book, to encourage me and pray us through this process. Your gift for tightening up the text without muting the message is a beautiful thing—and precisely that, a gift. Thank you for making sure my Ps and Qs are all as they should be. This book is all the better for having first passed through your hands.

My Blog readers, thank you for showing up, for leaving comments and sending emails. Thank you for the tweets, and texts and Facebook notes left out of love and kindness. You continue to inspire me with your generosity and friendship. Thank you for your support and for helping me see Jesus.

My friends and family, thank you for your help, both physically with the kids and emotionally, through your listening and through your prayers. You will never know the depths of my gratitude for your sacrifices of time and energy on my behalf. I am so deeply grateful.

Jesus, thank You certainly is too small a phrase for the One who died in my stead. This book is yours. I continue to be humbled by your grace and mercy. Thank you for allowing me to experience a tiny fraction of Lent, and your journey, to bring me closer to you. How gracious you are, to let me see you this way. My life forever remains in your love-pierced hands. *How great thou art.*

Additional Reading

The following is a list of additional resources that I used for both my own personal study and reflection in writing this book. This list is by no means exhaustive.

Reliving the Passion, Walter Wangerin
He Chose the Nails, Max Lucado
The Pursuit of the Holy: A Divine Invitation, Simon Ponsonby
Everything: What You Give and What You Gain to Become More Like Jesus, Mary DeMuth
The Cost of Discipleship, Deitrich Bonhoeffer
The Signature of Jesus: The Call to a Life Marked by Holy Passion and a Relentless Faith, Brennan Manning
All is Grace: A Ragamuffin Memoir, Brennan Manning
The Pursuit of God, A.W. Tozer
Circle of Seasons: Meeting God in the Church Year, Kimberly Conway Ireton
Valley of Vision: A Collection of Puritan Prayers & Devotions, Arthur G. Bennet
Hazardous: Committing to the Cost of Following Jesus, Ed Cyzewski and Derek Cooper
Glorious Ruin: How Suffering Sets You Free, Tullian Tchividjian

About The Author

Kris is a freelance writer with a passion for using her words to encourage, inspire, and lead others. She embraces the writing life while homeschooling her four children, and coordinating the MOPS ministry in her church. Kris also serves as an advocate for Compassion International which seeks to set children free from poverty in Jesus' name.

Her writing has been featured at **(in)Courage**, **Inspired To Action**, and contributes monthly to BibleDude.net and Allume.com. She blogs weekly at Always Alleluia.com and is a contributing author to the books, **Finding Church** (Civitas Press) and another upcoming project (yet to be titled) from Civitas Press, coming in March 2013).

Connect with Kris:
https://twitter.com/kriscamealy
https://www.facebook.com/krisecamealy
http://pinterest.com/kriscamealy
or email kris@alwaysalleluia.com

A Note About Compassion

<u>Compassion International</u> is a child development and advocacy ministry seeking to set children free from the bonds of poverty, in Jesus' name. Compassion is active in 26 countries around the world. Over 1.4 million children so far have been released from poverty, as they receive holistic care through the Compassion program. As an advocate for Compassion, I not only believe in the mission, but make every effort to participate through various campaigns, to help spread the message. By purchasing this book, you are partnering with me to help spread the message of hope in Christ, to others less fortunate than ourselves.

10% of each book purchased, will be donated back to Compassion International in an effort to continue the mission.
I am deeply grateful for your willingness to be a part of this ministry with me.

If a man shuts his ears to the cry of the poor,
he too will cry out and not be answered. *Proverbs 21:13*

Bonhoeffer, Dietrich. The Cost of Discipleship. London: SCM Press, 1948/2001.

Capon, Robert. The supper of the lamb : a culinary reflection. New York: Modern Library, 2002.

A Different Spirit. http://www.differentspirit.org/blog/gethsemane-and-what-follows/ December 2012.

Strong's Greek. http://biblesuite.com/greek/3340.htm December 2012.

Tozer, A.W. The pursuit of God. S.l: W_L_C, 2009.

Wangerin, Walter. Reliving the passion : meditations on the suffering, death, and resurrection of Jesus as recorded in Mark. Grand Rapids, Mich: Zondervan Pub. House, 1992.

14759295R00044

Printed in Poland
by Amazon Fulfillment
Poland Sp. z o.o., Wrocław